W9-AOA-102

Food Field Trips

Let's Explore Eggs!

Jill Colella

Lerner Publications ◆ Minneapolis

Hello Friends,

Everybody eats, even from birth. This is why learning about food is important. Making the right choices about what to eat begins with knowing more about food. Food literacy helps us to be more curious about food and adventurous about what we eat. In short, it helps us discover how delicious the world of food can be.

Eggs can be cooked many ways. When I was young, my Gran would make us eggs for breakfast. She made perfect little omelets in a small iron skillet. Stuffed with cheese, they tasted so good. How do you like your eggs?

For more inspiration, ideas, and recipes, visit www.teachkidstocook.com.

Jill

About the Author

Happy cook, reformed picky eater, and long-time classroom teacher, Jill Colella founded both *Ingredient* and *Butternut*, award-winning children's magazines that promote food literacy.

Lerner Publications Company
An imprint of Lerner Publishing Group, Inc.
241 First Avenue North
Minneapolis, MN 55401 USA

For reading levels and more information, look up this title at www.lernerbooks.com.

Main body text set in Mikado
Typeface provided by HVD

Library of Congress Cataloging-in-Publication Data
Names: Colella, Jill, author.
Title: Let's explore eggs! / Jill Colella.
Description: Minneapolis : Lerner Publications, 2020. | Series: Food field trips | Includes bibliographical references and index. | Audience: Ages 4–8 | Audience: Grades K–1 | Summary: "Eggs are delicious, nutritious, and versatile! Introduce young readers to the chickens and their farmers, learn to cook a simple egg and toast dish, then make plant pots from the shells"– Provided by publisher.
Identifiers: LCCN 2019052416 (print) | LCCN 2019052417 (ebook) | ISBN 9781541590373 (library binding) | ISBN 9781728402833 (paperback) | ISBN 9781728400204 (ebook)
Subjects: LCSH: Cooking (Eggs) | Eggs as food. | LCGFT: Cookbooks.
Classification: LCC TX745 .C65 20210 (print) | LCC TX745 (ebook) | DDC 641.6/75—dc23

LC record available at https://lccn.loc.gov/2019052416
LC ebook record available at https://lccn.loc.gov/2019052417

Manufactured in the United States of America
1 – CG – 7/15/20

SCAN FOR BONUS CONTENT!

Table of Contents

Picture Glossary

coop

hen

nest

shell

yolk

ALL ABOUT EGGS

Eggs are tasty on their own. They are also used to make other foods.

Eggs act like glue in noodles. Eggs also help cakes and other baked goods rise.

Have you made a recipe with eggs in it?

LET'S COMPARE

There are many ways to cook eggs. Have you tried eggs cooked these ways?

baked

hard-boiled

omelet

over easy

scrambled

sunny-side up

LET'S EXPLORE

An egg is made of different parts.

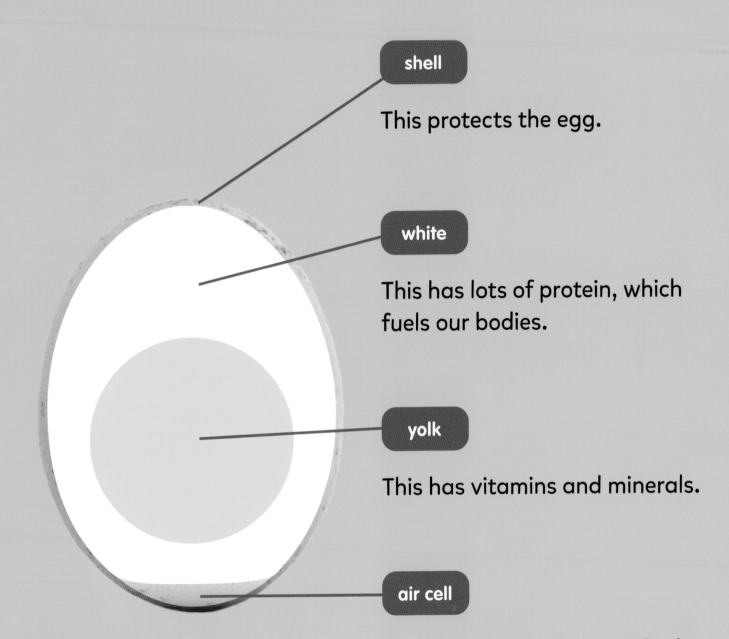

shell

This protects the egg.

white

This has lots of protein, which fuels our bodies.

yolk

This has vitamins and minerals.

air cell

This is a pocket of air inside the shell. It stores oxygen.

LET'S VISIT A HENHOUSE

Eggs come from chickens. Chickens that lay eggs are called hens.

Some hens live on farms.
Some live in backyards.

Look at this cozy house. It has
windows and a ramp.

This is called a chicken coop or henhouse.

What else does this henhouse have?

13

Chickens need food and water to grow. They eat grasses, weeds, and bugs.

They also eat fruits, vegetables, and grains.

Hens rest in their coops.
They sit on nests of hay
or straw.

Hens lay eggs in their
nests. A hen can lay about
one egg a day.

A farmer gathers the eggs. Many farmers sell their eggs.

How many eggs do you count?

It is time to cook and
bake with the eggs.
Thank you, hens!

LET'S COOK

Always have an adult present when working in the kitchen!

EGG-IN-TOAST

INGREDIENTS

- 1 slice of bread
- 1 teaspoon butter
- 1 egg
- salt and pepper

1. Use a circle cutter (or the rim of a juice glass) to punch a hole in the center of the slice of bread.

2. Melt the butter in a pan over medium heat.

3. Put the bread slice in the pan.

4. Crack the egg into a small bowl. Pour the egg into the hole in the bread.

5. Let the egg cook for 2 minutes.

6. Flip the bread and egg. Cook them for 2 to 4 more minutes.

7. Put your egg-in-toast onto a plate. Top it with salt and pepper.

SEE THIS RECIPE IN ACTION!

LET'S MAKE

Needles and awls are sharp!
Ask an adult for help.

EGGSHELL PLANT POTS

MATERIALS

- egg carton
- eggshell halves, rinsed clean
- knitting needle or awl
- spray bottle
- water
- seed starter mix or potting soil
- seeds for your favorite plant

1. Place the eggshell halves in the carton. Use the needle to gently make a hole in the bottom of each shell. This will allow water to drain out.

2. Spray some water into the eggshells. Then fill the shells with the seed starter mix or potting soil.

3. Plant the seeds in the soil and spray the soil with more water.

4. Place the egg carton in a sunny place. Spray the soil gently with water when it looks dry.

5. When the seedlings are large enough, gently crack the shell and plant it (and the seedling) in a pot or garden.

Let's Read

American Egg Board—Virtual Egg Farm Field Trips
https://www.aeb.org/eggs-in-schools/classroom/farm-to-table-virtual-field-trips

Hoffmann, Sara E. *Eggs*. Minneapolis: Lerner Publishing Group, 2014.

The Incredible Egg—On the Farm
https://www.incredibleegg.org/where-eggs-come-from/

Kids Learning Videos—Chickens!
https://www.youtube.com/watch?v=wYKJkHcaMzE

Kington, Emily. *I Am Not an Egg Carton!* Minneapolis: Hungry Tomato, 2019.

Tuminelly, Nancy. *Let's Cook with Eggs! Delicious & Fun Egg Dishes Kids Can Make*.
Minneapolis: ABDO Pub. Co., 2013.

Photo Acknowledgments

The images in this book are used with the permission of: © 4kodiak/iStockphoto, p. 7 (scrambled eggs); © Anastasiia Magonova/iStockphoto, pp. 3 (white hen), 10; © Ann_Zhuravleva/iStockphoto, p. 6 (baked egg); © binabina/iStockphoto, p. 17; © DebraMillet/iStockphoto, pp. 3, 12; © dirkr/iStockphoto, p. 7 (omelet); © Fotoatelie/iStockphoto, p. 5 (challah); © georgeclerk/iStockphoto, p. 16; © GMVozd/iStockphoto, pp. 3 (egg yolk), 4; © HONG VO/iStockphoto, p. 9; © JillLang/iStockphoto, p. 13; © KroXi/iStockphoto, p. 5 (pasta); © LauriPatterson/iStockphoto, p. 20; © MahirAtes/iStockphoto, pp. 3 (eggs isolated), 8; © martin-dm/iStockphoto, p. 18; © milanfoto/iStockphoto, p. 6; © monticelllo/iStockphoto, p. 14; © NikiLitov/iStockphoto, p. 19; © NikonShutterman/iStockphoto, p. 11 (chickens in field); © Pixavril/iStockphoto, p. 15; © Prostock-studio/Shutterstock Images, p. 5; © rjlerich/iStockphoto, p. 7 (egg on toast); © RyanJLane/iStockphoto, p. 15 (apples); © Sasiistock/iStockphoto, p. 23; © serts/iStockphoto, p. 1; © SimonSkafar/iStockphoto, p. 3 (brown hen in nest); © SolStock/iStockphoto, p. 11 (boy holding chicken); © ThitareeSarmkasat/iStockphoto, p. 22; © Tsuji/iStockphoto, p. 7; © twilightproductions/iStockphoto, p. 11; © vgajic/iStockphoto, p. 15 (boy feeding chicken); © VioletaStoimenova/iStockphoto, p. 21.

Cover Photos: © ahirao_photo/iStockphoto (pancakes and eggs); © georgeclerk/iStockphoto (white hen); © MahirAtes/iStockphoto; © martin-dm/iStockphoto (girl collecting eggs); © serts/iStockphoto (eggs in basket)